254

To
Professor Elmer G Homrighausen

with appreciation.

George Stoll.

LAYMEN AT WORK

LAYMEN AT WORK

"How to meet human needs in your town"

by GEORGE STOLL

edited by ALBERT L. MEIBURG

ABINGDON PRESS

NEW YORK • NASHVILLE

LAYMEN AT WORK

Copyright © MCMLVI by Abingdon Press

Library of Congress Catalog Card Number: 56-10150

SET UP, PRINTED, AND BOUND BY THE
PARTHENON PRESS, AT NASHVILLE,
TENNESSEE, UNITED STATES OF AMERICA

EDITOR'S PREFACE

The church population of America is on the increase, but so is the population of our prisons. More is being spent on education than ever before, but more and more juveniles are being arrested. What is the answer? Christ is the answer, but Christ works through men. What are the churches doing to mobilize their growing man power? Here is the story of what the churches of a typical city are doing.

In 1941 the Council of Churches of Louisville, Kentucky, was looking for a chairman for its Committee on Institutions. They chose George Stoll, a Methodist Sunday-school worker and oil-company executive. Mr. Stoll knew the challenge of institutional work from his first-hand experience as a "chronic board member." He also knew men. He brought his experience as a worker with men to bear on the problem. He knew the churches of his city. His service with the State Sunday School Association convinced him that the church man power needed to minister to public institutions was available, but unmobilized. Convinced that every Christian should find a personal task in the service of the kingdom of God, he found the work of his committee clearly outlined in Matt. 25:31-46: "I was sick, and ye visited me . . . in prison, and ye came unto me."

It is the hope of the men who have shared in it that

this experiment in Christian service may be an encouragement to others. It is not presented as the final answer to the problem of the church and community needs, but as a signpost pointing in the direction of an answer. If, as William Carey declared, we must expect great things from God, why not expect some great things from God's children?

Grateful acknowledgment is made to the following persons who have assisted in the preparation of this manuscript:

William H. Leach, senior editor of *Church Management,* graciously permitted the use of certain stories from a column by Mr. Stoll which appeared in the magazine beginning in 1953.

Henry Noble Sherwood, G. S. Dobbins, and Wayne E. Oates, all of Louisville, have given valuable help and encouragement.

One does not deal lightly with thoughts and experiences that are literally the offspring of a personality passionately devoted to the kingdom of God. It is, therefore, with some measure of fear and trembling that I present this arrangement of stories compiled from Mr. Stoll's speeches, articles, and personal memoranda. My earnest hope is that the zeal of the men described here may strike fire in the hearts of many other laymen who, after all, *are* the church.

ALBERT L. MEIBURG

INTRODUCTION

Some Christians are so eager to be the light of the world that they forget the necessity of working quietly like the salt of the earth. Not so with the laymen of the Committee on Institutions of the Louisville Council of Churches. They have worked quietly, pervasively, and redemptively in the life of their city. I myself have been blessed by these men who are at work day and night not being ministered unto but ministering, according to their Master's command (Matt. 20:28). I observed them in action when I was a theological student at the Southern Baptist Theological Seminary. I participated with them as a chaplain and as a pastor in the community of Louisville. Now they help me in the process of teaching my students in my class and field work as a professor of pastoral care in my Alma Mater.

The main message of this book is to tell the story of these men at work, to clarify the moving purposes, guiding methodology, and basic philosophy of what D. Elton Trueblood has called their "other vocation." The book, written by George Stoll, the man who conceived the original plan of action, and edited by Albert Meiburg, who has made an over-all study of the program himself, is written in plain English, free of the gobbledegook that fills many supposedly weightier tomes. The book speaks plainly, realistically, and tenderly of the heart needs of the dispossessed people of the streets and institutions of an average American city. God is at work revealing himself here to men where the Lord Jesus Christ promised them that he could be seen by those who have eyes to see.

Here is set forth a plan addressed not only to the needs of inmates of institutions, offenders of the laws of society, and the growing lives of parentless people. This book also speaks to the need of laymen in the churches for an answer to their own sense of meaninglessness, pointlessness, and boredom with life. Having spent the fore part of their lives in the struggle to establish themselves in their work and to provide for their families, adult men in the churches often begin to experience the tediousness and tastelessness of life. The routine of their work has been mastered and its challenge often levels off into "just another day's work." The excitement of growing children is no longer available to many of them because their children have left home. Even the attendance upon church can be just one more meeting to attend, a chore to do, and more of the "same old stuff."

The patterns of meaning and action set forth in the pages of this book speak with a new vitality to these needs of adult men. The empty places of real men's lives have been filled, the desert places of spiritual unproductivity have been made fertile and abounding, and the meaning of life has become clear afresh to men who by means of the comfort wherewith they have been comforted of God have become a comfort to those who are in any affliction (II Cor. 1:4).

I heartily commend these men's lives, and this book which is a record of their lives, as a "living epistle" to be read by men who seriously hunger for fresh adventure in the kingdom of God.

WAYNE E. OATES

Professor of Psychology of Religion and Pastoral Care Southern Baptist Theological Seminary

CONTENTS

1

Men at Work

The parole board was meeting at Eddyville, Kentucky. They brought in an old prisoner.

"John, why don't you ask for a parole?" asked the chairman.

"Who, me?" replied John. "I have no place to go. All my people are dead, and no one would give a man like me a job anymore. I'd have no place to go."

He turned and started to leave. Then he said, "May I speak?"

"Say anything you want," said the chairman.

"I am a dead man," John said. "You're looking at a ghost. There's nothing you can do for me. But you *can* do something for the boys who are here. I hear them turning on their cots at night. I hear them weep. I hear them pray God to do something for them. You can do something for those boys."

With this, John turned and left. The board was silent for quite a time.

What would you have done if you had been on the board? Of course, parole boards can't turn boys out of prison because they weep, or even because they pray. But there are things that can be done for boys in prison, for children in child-care agencies, and for patients in hospitals. Here are some examples of what happens when experts and laymen work together to see what can be done for people in trouble.

For example, there is the story of how some prominent churchmen in Louisville found themselves in police court. There they got a glimpse of what was happening to the ten thousand persons arrested by their city police each year. Of course, they were not "guests" in custody, only informal observers. But their observations and reactions spearheaded a significant movement in the religious and civic life of their city.

The case of the churchmen in court goes back to fifteen years ago when the Committee on Institutions of the Louisville Council of Churches asked a group of churches in a given locale to study the police court. Each of the pastors was asked to bring three or four hand-picked laymen to represent his church in the creation of a police-court committee.

Pretty early in the game the men felt a need to get some firsthand impressions of what the court was like. That's how they wound up in the police holdover!

With the co-operation of the court they set up a round-the-clock visit to the booking desk one week end, when they knew things would be busy. There they saw a flesh-and-blood drama. One of the men set down his impressions in the following way:

Sunday Morning

I have just spent four hours at the booking desk of the city police holdover. I arrived at a quarter to twelve Saturday night and left at a quarter to four Sunday morning.

The police major graciously introduced me to all the officers, who gave me a friendly welcome. The fine spirit of camaraderie among the police was extended to me in more than a formal sense, so that I felt accepted as a member in good standing.

I saw sights to make angels weep.

I saw youngsters caught stealing cars—out for a joy ride that took them to jail. An officer said that over half the car thefts in our town were attributed to minors.

I saw a shivering young girl, evidently held on a morals charge, clad in a thin skirt and blouse. She was herded with others in the 10 degree cold into a patrol wagon for the trip to the county jail. She shrieked: "If they send me out there, I will kill myself!" I thought the officer took it rather nonchalantly, but he told me in an aside that she had been "out there" before.

Mostly I saw alcoholics. There was one fat man dead drunk who must have weighed over three hundred pounds. Officers had to drag him down the steps and corridor to the holdover. He lay on the floor and was slated as John Doe until he could recover and give his correct identification.

I saw a woman, whose appearance implied culture and advantage, drunk and trying to dial friends. She was too far gone to be successful until after many attempts. I asked permission to help her but was told that definite orders prohibited anyone in the holdover room except police and prisoners. The reason for this was to protect bystanders.

I later learned that the woman held an important position in the city, but she was an alcoholic and every now and then suffered one of these mishaps. After a while a well-dressed man came and arranged bail for her and took her away.

They were all herded in, young and old, black and white, prostitutes and traffic violators, gamblers, thieves and drunks. Some were weeping, some asking for help, most were hazy from the effects of drinking. It seemed to me that the church, the representative of Christ on earth, should have been there to counsel and guide, to be the friend in need, and to find a way to prevent this open sore on the body of society. Were the church to spend as much money on such a study as it spends on inspiring music, would not the inspirational value be equal in knowing that we were serving "the least of these"?

Such sights of human life and want in the raw prompted the men to learn more about the court, which is the first one to deal with an arrested person. Relatively minor cases involving such misdemeanors as disorderly conduct may be tried in this court. More serious cases, felonies, are referred to a higher court where trial by jury is the rule. Some cases may be dismissed or filed away. The police court tries to give a prompt review to the cases of all persons arrested and to dispose of the charges or assign the case to a higher court. This is quite a task, and a particularly burdensome one in cities where there are thousands of arrests annually.

When booking is completed, the person usually attempts to secure his release on bond, so as to avoid being put in jail. Usually he must depend upon the services of a professional bondsman to arrange surety. The bondsman charges the arrested person a fee proportionate to the amount of bond required, for which the bondsman agrees to be liable in case the arrested person fails to appear for trial.

The activity of these bondsmen was a chronic handicap to the court and to the police department. This was one of the first problems confronted by the committee. They invited well-posted officials of the court to tell them in their monthly meetings about the activities of these bondsmen. There were such stories as the one of the country boy who came to town, took a few drinks, ran a red light, and was arrested. The bondsman frightened him by making his offense appear extremely serious, while at the same time offering him escape from the situation at an exorbitant rate.

The answer to this sort of problem doesn't jump out and strike you down. But real men facing real issues have to contend with discouraging odds and appearances. This is true of progress in any human endeavor. So the laymen of the committee supported and encouraged the officials who wanted to supervise bondsman practices. Those who work in this court now say that bondsman activity is much better controlled.

In the course of time the laymen got to know the chief of police, the chief of detectives, the director of crime prevention, the clerk of the court, the prosecutor, and the safety commissioner.

Certain problems of the court came under the co-operative scrutiny of officials and laymen alike—such as, the matter of a large percentage of traffic tickets "filed away," and the problem of the sale of obscene literature in the city. Although not every problem studied was "solved" forthwith, at least two things did happen: (1) a good number of church-minded citizens became vitally concerned about what went on at the police court, and (2) the general level of the conduct of the court improved.

Beginning in 1941 with the formation of this police-court group, the Committee on Institutions has grown until now men are "at work" on thirteen such groups, each related to some institution in or near the city. The Penal Division includes the committees on the police court, the criminal court, the jail, and the state reformatory. The Health Division is composed of committees on the general hospital, the chronic-disease hospital, the state tuberculosis sanatorium, and the state mental hospital. The Child-Care Division is formed by committees on the boys' club, the juvenile court, crime prevention, the state children's home, and the county children's home.

2

A Funeral for "They"

A favorite American indoor sport is "passing the buck." *They* ought to do something about our schools. *They* ought to clean up the mess in Washington. *They* ought to lower taxes. It seems that *they* is a big culprit.

A business firm held a funeral for *they*. Everyone from manager to janitor attended the funeral. Someone fixed up a box for a casket. In it was placed *they*. And the whole organization buried *they*. Henceforth and forever, no one of them could say, "*They* ought to do something about it"—*they* was dead. No doubt about it. *They* was buried. No longer would the villain roam about neglecting responsibilities, making mistakes, passing up messes that should be cleaned up, overlooking things which needed to be done. *They* had ceased to exist. *They* was dead and buried.

All the business, jobs, and responsibilities of *They, Them, and Company* became the business, jobs, and responsibilities of *We, Us, and Company*.

This story pulses with meaning for Christian men.

With this funeral over, "*They* should do something about it" becomes "*We* should do something about it."

"*They* should produce, elect, and support good officials" becomes "*We* should produce, elect, and support good officials."

"*They* should visit the sick and imprisoned, the widowed and the fatherless" becomes "*We* should visit the sick and imprisoned, the widowed and the fatherless."

"*They* should be doers of the word, not hearers only" becomes "*We* should be doers of the word, not hearers only."

Let's all bury *they*.

A unique emphasis in the work of the men of the Committee on Institutions has been to spread the idea that it is the business of the church to furnish good men for public institutions, then to support, not criticize them.

The experience of the Jail Committee illustrates how overcoming evil with good is practical!

When the Jail Committee was first organized, the chairman of the Committee on Institutions suggested the adoption of a policy of *no adverse public criticism*.

One man said to him, "I guess you won't criticize the jailer."

"No," he said, "I'm not going to criticize him."

At that the man turned away with a sort of wise look on his face, implying, "Well, maybe he will learn, and maybe he is just hopeless." That chap just knew that the only thing that would do any good was criticism.

"Now, if criticism would have helped that jail," said the chairman, "it certainly would have had a lot of help, for there had been much criticism. There were all sorts of stories in the newspapers. Rumors were thick. And here was a bunch of harebrained idealists who were not going to criticize!"

The chairman made the first contact himself. He got one politician to introduce him to another politician who introduced him to the jailer. He remarked, "I was well introduced, vouched for by mutual friends." He told the jailer about the committee and that they had pledged themselves to a policy of no unfavorable public criticism of the management of the institution.

"We will not divulge any confidence we receive in our attempts to support and aid the jail," he said.

This was new language!

He also told the jailer that the group was sponsoring no reform wave. They were more interested in the long pull. They wanted to learn what, if anything, they could do to help.

Four or five hand-picked men from each of four churches were asked to pray ten times daily, "Thy kingdom come—and let me help." The men were asked to read the twenty-fifth chapter of Matthew and to remember that Jesus said, "I was in prison, and ye came unto me." In preparation for the monthly discussion meetings they read the professional literature on jail management to learn the current trends in this field. How were jails handled in other cities? What was paid for food? How long did the inmate stay in jail? What was done to help the inmate come out a better person than he went in?

The things that began to happen at the jail are a story to themselves. The committee itself didn't do it. The jailer made the improvements. Meeting with it for study gave him some ideas, but most of all some encouragement.

On another occasion in one state a committee learned privately that the inmates of the institution it was studying were being mishandled. The rumor sounded serious. What should be done? What should be said?

23

Several committeemen decided to arrange an interview with the administrator. There was a strained silence. Then one of the laymen spoke:

"See here! I'd hate to run an institution and have Tom, Dick, and Harry always asking me what we did and why. All I ask you is when people ask *us* about it, what'll we tell them?"

The institutional head looked relieved. He smiled. "I'll tell you fellows anything," he said. He explained all about it. It didn't seem quite so bad when you had all the facts. Still, it was bad enough. Then he said, "And it will never happen again."

Thoughtless criticism is one of the most serious occupational hazards faced by public servants. A part of the work of the Committee on Institutions has been to find ways of reducing the occupational hazards confronting men who work for the public. Suppose the matter mentioned above had been dragged through the papers and the official put on the defensive. Would his pledge have been obtained? Yet here was a promise freely given and given with appreciation.

The Mental-Hospital Committee also saw a need for positive support and encouragement of public officials. "What can we do about this?" they began to ask one another.

One man gave his opinion.

"As I see it," he said, "these staff people are really employees of the taxpaying public, since they work for the state. In my business I try to encourage my employees to do their very best. I think we as a part of the public can find some way to do that."

The committee hit upon the idea of a recognition dinner for the whole hospital staff from the doctors to the aides. Ladies of a church agreed to serve the meal. Some local leaders in government agreed to attend. The committee expressed its appreciation for the work of this staff and had them make the talks at the dinner. The staff was very appreciative and the committee repeated the dinner for several years.

Another state hospital, hearing of the work of this committee, asked it to make a visit to their institution. Accordingly, several cars of laymen went by appointment to this other hospital. The trip required an overnight visit. The committee found the hospital in fine physical condition. A good job was being done. It didn't see that there was anything it could do.

Then it was told that the hospital wanted to put in facilities for music therapy. The equipment needed would cost $2,500. What money the committee had was already allocated in its work. However, one member of the committee had an idea. He knew of an employee organization of a large business firm that had taken an interest in this kind of thing before. He laid the need before that organization and it provided the money for the equipment.

Shortly after this happened the committeeman died. The officials of the hospital were so appreciative of the job he had done that they invited the committee to attend the unveiling of a bronze plaque placed in the hospital in memory of what one layman had done. He saw a need. He found a way to use the resources of the community to meet that need.

There are many such things which any group of concerned laymen can do if it is willing to spend a bit of time and effort in study. Needs will be uncovered. Ways to meet these needs can be found.

In almost every meeting of any of the groups of the Committee on Institutions there will be a mention of its "One Rule." The rule: "There will be no unfavorable public criticism of the management of any institution we study and seek to serve." The successful keeping of many confidences has attested the committee's willingness to abide by this rule, which Horace B. Ward, writing for the Associated Press, called "perhaps the chief reason for the committee's success."

As the chairman puts it:

We, the people, have been a poor employer. A good employer endeavors to ENCOURAGE AND SUPPORT.

No one likes criticism. In the case of the public's criticism of institutions, it is often politically inspired and unfair. Let's never have it said in the future that the only word public officials hear from churchmen's groups is criticism.

When management realizes you are not a snooping section, but a cheering section, management tells you its problems; invites your help. (A team plays better with a cheering section.) The rule creates confidence and good will. Management is encouraged to do its best, knowing that friends are observing—for management is human too.

3

Getting the Facts

"Gentlemen, I have been judge of this court for five years and this is the first time any group of Christian men has ever asked me to tell them anything about it."

The county judge, who was also the juvenile court judge, was speaking to a committee of laymen who represented churches from one neighborhood. He was a fine-looking man and made a fine talk about the court. In the course of his remarks he made the further statement: "This court ought not to be under the county judge. This court ought to be out of politics, and the county judge is politics from inside to outside." The men had not realized what a fine man the county judge was. They had not realized that he would suggest such a progressive move. But they were smart enough to back him up.

They were smart enough, too, to realize that before they could give support to progressive men and policies they must have accurate information. Perhaps one reason why institutional managers are sometimes wary of volunteer lay assistance is that they fear what uninformed or misinformed people may do. It is well to mean well, but good intentions are not enough. There is no substitute for the facts.

The visit of the county judge to the Juvenile Court

Committee illustrates that lay groups may get hold of the facts. Responsible men in institutions and government welcome the opportunity to tell interested and sympathetic citizens the story of their agencies—especially when they understand that they are not being put on the spot.

If you put yourself into the position of an institutional head for a moment, you can understand the "coaching" philosophy of this approach. Suppose a group of substantial, intelligent people had taken the trouble to become accurately informed about your institution. Suppose in a friendly way they recognized you and asked you to tell them, as interested people who appreciated what you were doing, about your work. Wouldn't this make you strive to do your best? Isn't it natural for a man to seek the approval of a group who knows something about his field?

Reading the best current literature in a given field is another way to get the facts. At first many men feel lost in trying to help a specialized agency such as a hospital or prison or juvenile court when there are trained persons already at work.

When the Jail Committee read *Alcoholics Anonymous,* they saw the baffling as well as the hopeful side of the problem of many jail inmates. When the Prison Committee shared *Prisons and Beyond* by Sanford Bates, they were challenged to believe that there is a better, if as yet undiscovered, alternative to prison. Lay groups which are willing to give time to the serious study of chapters of books and articles from standard professional journals will find that this is a profitable way to get the facts. And having the facts will not diminish at all their standing in the eyes of "the experts."

The Louisville groups have found comparative surveys helpful. They try to discover what allied groups in the same field are doing. In studying ways to prevent juvenile crime, they got acquainted with the work of the Boy Scouts, the Big Brother movement, and the Boys Clubs of America. The Jail Committee kept in touch with the state commission which was planning an alcoholic-treatment center. Some of the men who occasionally travel on business have visited courts and prisons in other states to compare procedures.

At times the men have carried their search for the facts into the institution itself. For example, the Police Court Committee was able to arrange a schedule of visits to enable its members to see the police in action. Some men spent an evening in a police cruiser on routine patrol. Meanwhile, other men observed in the city-hospital emergency room, the booking room, the interrogation room, and the crime prevention bureau. By taking turns at the various centers of activity on successive nights, the group gained a wonderfully enlightening firsthand impression of how the police operate. Just riding with the vice squad one night is a revelation.

The Jail Committee also did some field study along this line. They had been meeting monthly with the jailer, wondering how they might be of help to him.

One night the men asked if they might arrange to visit the jail in teams, so as to get a more comprehensive idea of how things worked. The jailer agreed. On Saturday night they began a vigil. At ten o'clock two laymen arrived, to be relieved by two others later, so that some members of the group were on hand from ten o'clock Saturday night until eight o'clock Monday morning. The officers at the jail co-operated. They allowed the laymen to see the situation just as it was. It was an interesting sight to see people brought to jail—interesting, but not edifying. It fired the spirits of those men to do something about it.

So the committee of laymen met together to combine its experiences at the jail. It called on each man around the circle to give his impressions and suggest possible ways in which the group might assist those in charge. Then it asked the jailer to give his views.

Things began to improve at the jail. The committee had taken little specific action. Directly it had done little. The jailer made the improvements. Joining in the study and discussion with the friendly circle of laymen had brought some things more clearly to his mind.

About that time an election rolled around. Both parties had nominated a candidate for jailer. It is not unusual for candidates to be invited to address civic groups such as women's clubs during their campaigns. The efforts of such groups are often directed so as to get the candidates pledged to support a good program: "Mr. Candidate, if you are elected what will you do about this?" or "Mr. Candidate, if you are elected what will you do about that?"

The committee, likewise, invited both candidates to meet with it, one at a time. But it made an entirely different approach. It said something like this to each candidate at separate meetings:

Mr. Candidate, we don't make any bones about saying what we think the jail needs. We feel that it needs a

30

cleanup and a program. We think that recreation and a library ought to be provided. We think the prisoners need some activity and some counseling. We think there should be a full-time chaplain directing a religious program.

But while we think there are plenty of things a jail ought to have, we want to say to you that we are not asking you to pledge to accomplish one single thing. If you are elected jailer, you are going to be the jailer. And if there is anything we can do to back you up or to assist you, call on us.

Now a strange thing happened. The committee didn't pledge the candidate to a thing. Yet everything it thought desirable for the jail appeared on the new jailer's program. He cleaned up that jail so that it didn't look like the same place. He picked a competent inmate to serve as librarian.

The laymen were able to help him contact the head of the psychology department at the local university. A group of students and a supervisor were sent to inaugurate group counseling.

A recreation program got under way. Eventually arrangements were made for the inmates to make furniture to be used by the city welfare department. The laymen checked with the retail merchants to see if there were any objections to this. "That's a good idea," the merchants said. "What can we do to help?" Then they asked the labor unions if they had any criticism. "No," they said, "it's all right. How can we help?"

Finally the jailer came to the laymen's group and asked, "What about that chaplain you mentioned?"

The group asked, "Can you pay him?"

"Sure," he said, "I'll make him a guard."

That's how the county jail secured one of the most

valuable deputy sheriffs it has ever had! The chaplain who was secured possessed a winning personality. He had a kindly spirit accompanied by mature judgment. His practical, firm, sympathetic nature won him a place in the affections of the inmates. You can imagine the feelings of the Jail-Committee men when he reported to them one evening, "I had four conversions this week, and I think two of them are genuine."

This true story shows what men can do when they are willing first to *get the facts* and then *do something about the facts.* A seminary professor suggested the motto: "No action without study; no study without action."

4

The Least of These

On a visit to the prison the dean of a nearby school of social work and a layman from the Prison Committee were startled to hear the sounds of children's voices. "What could small children be doing here?" they asked.

The voices were coming from the interview rooms where inmates were receiving visits from their families. A glance into the room showed two young men talking through the separating screens to the two young women apparently their wives. One young woman was in tears. The other's face was etched with the lines of despair.

As the dean and his friend continued down the corridor, they wondered: could it be that the two young inmates were among the number who need not be in prison—if enough people worried about what might be done to "the least of these"?

Keeping "the least of these" out of prison was one of the goals of the Criminal-Court Committee. During one of its meetings when discussion centered on this matter, the commonwealth attorney spoke up and said, "Look here, I'll tell you something that you fellows can do to prevent crime. If some of you would serve as volunteer probation officers, I could probate some of these boys to you, and I believe we could avoid having them go to prison to become confirmed criminals. We should be able to salvage quite a few of them."

Six or seven members of the committee volunteered that evening. Soon they became acquainted with their boys. At the meetings they'd say, "*My* boy." "My boy isn't really a bad boy. If you had a prostitute for a mother and a drunkard for a father, what would happen to you?" They kept in touch with their boys and kept many out of further trouble. A wonderful contribution to the welfare of the communities could be made if laymen everywhere would try to help one "boy" do well!

In studying questions related to probation and parole some of the lawyers on this committee found that the statutes needed revising. They studied the model act prepared by the National Probation and Parole Association. Long hours were spent in conferences with state officials responsible for probation. Other hours were spent in writing revisions of the existing penal code so as to give the judge more opportunity to probate men if the circumstances of the case warranted. The governor was consulted and gave his approval to the proposed legislation so that it became an "administrative measure." All these revisions did not finally receive legislative approval, but *some did*. Changing laws so as to give more men a chance to make good is one way Christian men can use their professional skills in the service of the Kingdom.

But what if professional skills are lacking? Not every group of willing workers has the know-how to write legislation, or to do the thousand other things that wait to be done. Here the church and civic groups need to remember that they do not work in a social vacuum. The Lord still has many "who have not bowed the knee to the image of Baal" and who are willing to be enlisted. So when Christian action groups run into specialized problems, frequently they can secure competent assistance from community resource people—social workers, public-health workers, county agricultural agents, teachers in schools and colleges, doctors, men of experience in various fields of business.

This was certainly the case at the prison. The Prison Committee found problems which called for more specialized vocational abilities than its group numbered. So it searched out men of experience in certain lines of work who were glad to give some time.

For instance, one of the first matters dealt with at the prison involved food. The inmates were dissatisfied. Realizing that food is an important morale factor and that rows over food often touch off prison riots, the laymen consulted the warden. He welcomed a suggestion by one committeeman that they ask the help of one of the city's best cafeteria managers. This man made a tour of the prison kitchen and showed how the menu could be made more appetizing. This helped the situation greatly.

But although the cafeteria manager helped solve one problem, he raised another.

"Your diet here lacks vitamins," he said. "You should be getting more produce from your farm."

So the committee began to study the operation of the prison farm. The manager was doing a good job, but he had a problem in the handling of root vegetables. Another committeeman knew a retired, successful farmer who was well acquainted with crops. Any forward-looking man appreciates the opportunity to learn from men in his own field. The farm manager was pleased when this retired farmer suggested some ways to increase production and reduce spoilage. We can't say how much the committeemen's encouragement meant in this instance, but in a few years that farm which had been raising 37 per cent of the prison's food had moved production up to 67 per cent! Jesus said, "I was an hungred, and ye gave me meat."

At one prison there had been a prison newspaper called *The Rehabilitator*. Interest had lagged and it became defunct. As a matter of fact, *The Rehabilitator* was in great need of rehabilitation itself! An Associated Press writer known to another layman agreed to help the inmates get it going.

Needed improvements can be made by prison authorities if they have the co-operation and encouragement of interested laymen. Outside help can be enlisted.

A volunteer group similar to the Prison Committee was formed in another state and began working with the inmates of a woman's prison. They found the women idle—and consequently very unhappy. What to do?

After studying the situation, the group found a chance to build a worth-while program. They went downtown and talked to wholesalers who donated some bolts of cloth out of their slower moving stocks. They secured some secondhand sewing machines inexpensively and some thread and other accessories. Some of the women in that prison were mothers. They had children at home. The women were overjoyed to be able to make clothes for their children. In fact this project helped to create a new attitude at that institution. Some of the women who weren't mothers sewed for nephews and nieces. Some made Christmas presents. The sewing project shed a new light on the words of Jesus in Matt. 25:36, "When I had no clothes, you gave me clothes" (Goodspeed).

A woman's group was organized to help out at the women's prison. As they put on recreational and inspirational programs, they became acquainted with one particular inmate who seemed especially lonely. An unmarried mother, she brought forth her child in the prison and thought that no one cared. When the woman's group brought a layette for the little baby who had arrived in such grim surroundings, the mother broke down and wept. It was the first time she had been known to weep while in confinement. The fact that someone did care produced a constructive change in her life.

"The least of these" often shows a surprising insight into his own need for self-understanding. A member of the Prison Committee observed this while visiting a prison in a neighboring state. He came to a row of cells where the men were so dangerous and so feared that the guards were not allowed to fully open the door to furnish their food. There was a heavy chain which let the door open just so far. A white line was painted down the corridor about five feet from the cells and posted notices warned people not to cross that line.

The layman asked the warden if he might cross that line and talk to one of the men. Permission was given. He went over to one of the cells and saw a fine muscular youth inside. "Fine football material," he said to himself.

Then he said to the boy, "Son, I want to ask a favor of you. There's a group of men visiting here from the churches of the city. I wonder if you could give us any ideas on what a group of men like ours could do for the boys here?"

The boy thought a minute. Then he said, "Well, I'll tell you. I believe it would help a lot if we could have a psychiatrist."

That from murderers' row!

Sometimes the "least of these" is not a law violator but the average American citizen. After all, the law ultimately depends on the citizen for its enforcement. The exaggerated feeling of his own unimportance seems to hinder the citizen from performing his functions efficiently. Take the grand jury, for instance. Few citizens relish the prospect of jury service, to say the least.

Perhaps this is due in part to a lack of appreciation for the real importance of the grand jury in American government. It is one of those safety devices to protect the rights of the individual. But such devices require man power. The ways of the court sometimes appear cumbersome and fraught with undue delay. For instance, a man commits a murder. The murder is witnessed by responsible citizens. There is no question about the murderer's guilt, but he cannot even be tried by a petit, or trial, jury until the case has been examined by a grand, or investigating, jury. In this way citizens are protected from hasty and unfair accusation or conviction.

If the grand jury indicts, the man must then be tried by a petit jury and he must be defended. If he does not have a lawyer, the court appoints one. The defense lawyer has the right to challenge and take off the jury panel more jurors than the prosecution can remove.

Getting back to the jury itself, the truth is that grand juries are made up of average, and often above-average, citizens seeking to do a good job; but they are inexperienced and unfamiliar with legal processes.

The judge of the court in Louisville saw the need and gave a fine lecture to each jury. But how much of one lecture can a person retain?

The Criminal-Court Committee, composed of laymen from churches in one of the residential areas of the city, included six lawyers, one of whom was a teacher in a law school. They studied what other states do. They learned that New York publishes a manual for the use of jurors. But New York laws differ from Kentucky laws. After reading the New York manual, the committee decided to write one that would be suitable for its own state.

When this manual was ready to print, copies were submitted to the court, the prosecuting attorney, the bar association, and various civic and religious groups. It was printed under the title *Helps for Grand Jurors in Kentucky,* edited by Charles E. Keller. It received the endorsement of B'nai B'rith, the League of Catholic Parent-Teacher Associations, the Louisville Bar Association, the Louisville Council of Jewish Women, the League of Women Voters, and the Louisville Urban League.

The chairman of the Penal Division of the Committee on Institutions, Charles Keller, is himself a lawyer. He did most of the work of preparing the manual and he sees that the proper officials get a supply of manuals at the proper time. Each citizen summoned for grand-jury service is given a copy of the manual by the deputy serving the summons. Thus each citizen has an opportunity to know what his duties, authority, and responsibilities are before he reports to the court for service.

The following excerpts from the manual give some idea as to its usefulness:

If you are one who seeks to avoid jury service, remember this: the grand jury is the unique American heritage protecting every one of us from standing trial for a crime until at least nine on a grand jury of our fellow Americans say there is unexplained evidence which makes it appear likely the accused has committed a crime. Would *you* wish to stand public trial before there has been a fair hearing of your probable guilt? Would *you* wish to bear the expense and worry of a defense against a frivolous charge? The grand jury is the system which protects people from being prosecuted under false charges unless a group of citizens has heard a complaining witness support the claim that is made.

Remember: Today you are the person selected as a grand juror to pass upon the rights of others, but tomorrow you may be accused. If you do not make the system work today, it may not be here for you tomorrow.

The grand jury has another unique function in this republic of ours—it watches our officials in the way they serve us. We have been reasonably careful to vote for good men, but democracy does not stop there. The next step is to learn whether those men are doing the jobs they were elected to do. Most of them are, but unfortunately not all our officials honestly do the work they were elected or appointed to do. The grand jury is that group of citizens chosen to see that these officials do their job and to see that our public institutions such as prisons, public hospitals and homes for the aged are being operated not for the superintendents but for the public and the inmates. The function of a grand jury goes even further—it makes recommendations for the improvement of our public institutions.

Active grand juries are a guard against any alliance of crime and politics. Interested service by intelligent citizens makes an active grand jury. That is your contribution to government; this is your opportunity.[1]

The acceptance of the manual has been noteworthy. The county has taken more interest in the jury. The jury has taken more interest in itself. As a later development the commonwealth's attorney addressed a special meeting of the civics teachers of the county high schools and they adopted the manual as a teaching aid for their classes.

The Criminal-Court group has plans on foot for the future. It hopes to encourage the establishment of a city penal farm similar to those in Atlanta and Memphis. If at some future time there is a merger of city and county governments, a host of problems will arise for the jail and its administration. In good times and bad there is plenty to be done by willing, dedicated men.

Have you considered "the least of these" in your community?

[1] Used by permission of the Louisville Area Council of Churches.

5

An Ounce of Prevention

The Black Maria was taking the prisoners to the workhouse. From one of the diamond-shaped air holes a man's hand reached out as if groping for something. Just a hand—a human hand—reaching—for what? Did the man expect someone to reach out a hand in response?

When he was a very small boy, he could hold up his dimpled, pudgy hand and someone would take hold of it and help him over the rough places, through the hard experiences. He could reach up his hand, but now—?

Did his mind go back along the years? Did he remember the time he was playing in the yard and fell? His father saw him crying and came out, and the lad reached up his hand—

Did this seem like that horrible dream he had when he cried out in the night and his mother came in? When he reached out his hand, she picked him up and held him close and comforted him and made him feel secure again. Did he expect to find some way out of this nightmare of a life he had been living?

He reached out his hand. For what? For whom? Whose job is this?

Is it a job only for the warden at the workhouse, or

could it be a job for a Sunday-school teacher as well? Is it a job for the social worker, or could it suggest a job for a Christian businessman to tackle too?

Of course, the immediate needs of the man on his way to the workhouse are important, and in the preceding chapter we have seen how men can be mobilized to do something about folks in trouble. But how did it happen that this man was arrested in the first place? What lines of personal or social disaster were concluded as he faced the judge? What can be done by people who care to prevent the same circumstances from arising again for this man or for others?

You see, finding ways to help people *after* they are in our jails and hospitals is relatively easy. The real teaser is finding ways to prevent their having to go there in the first place. In other words there are long-term aspects as well as immediate aspects of the problems of disease and crime.

Take juvenile delinquency, for example.

You can't read a paper without finding some expert's opinion on the causes.

But frankly, what has *your* church done about the problem in *your* community? After all, that's where the battle will be won—at the grass roots.

The Juvenile-Court Committee set up a subgroup to find ways of preventing juvenile crime in its town. The chairman of the subcommittee gave the thing serious and sober thought, but he didn't let the odds get him down.

Living in his home was a social worker. He talked to her about it.

"How can you tell which kids will end up in court?" he asked her.

"Oh, we know kids who will go to juvenile court," she said.

"What have they done?" asked the chairman.

"Nothing yet."

"Well, what could we do that might keep these boys out of trouble?"

She thought a moment. "You might send some of them to camp."

That year the committee—not a single really rich church represented on it—sent 72 boys to camp. Each year after that they sent boys. The number more than doubled.

One night a member came to the meeting with this explosive comment: "We are on the wrong track completely."

"What do you mean 'wrong track'?"

"We are sending boys from the East End to camp. In their neighborhood they have the Wesley House to serve them. Near our own West-End neighborhood there's a place where the kids have no help at all."

What the man said was true. Not far away was an area in which there had been ninety-one arrests for juvenile delinquency in six blocks in six months. What to do?

The committee surveyed the area. Right in the middle of it they discovered a large building in which a church had maintained a community house. But it had been closed. They visited this church, talked over their aims, and the church gladly rented them the building for one dollar a year.

Then they asked the Community Chest if the Chest could maintain a program for boys in the house. The Chest said they could furnish a worker, but they could not furnish the money to fix up the church's building, nor could they furnish equipment. So the committee raised the money and the elbow grease for repairing and equipping the house. The Chest, through the Salvation Army, provided a worker whose name was Skelton. The boys called him "Red Skelton." That didn't hurt. They had their boys' club.

The next six months after that boys' club started, there was not a single arrest in that six-block area for juvenile crime. Score: 91 to 0! Not a bad try at preventing juvenile crime.

So far as the city as a whole goes, of course, the Committee on Institutions has been only one of many groups at work on the problem. It would be just as unfair to say that it did it all as to say that it did nothing.

The whole city has an enviable record of being freer than most towns from the epidemic of juvenile crime. And if church people can do something about preventing juvenile delinquency, what about adult delinquency? It seems that even fewer churches have a sense of responsibility for the grown-up lawbreaker than for the youngster gone wrong.

Consider the plight of the "nuisance drunks." A recent newspaper article estimated that a thousand or so compulsive drinkers cost the city of Louisville $465,000 a year! The figure was based on the fact that it costs $45 to arrest, book, try, and jail each of the thirty or so alcoholics who stumble out of police cars each day.

Some pathetic tales are told of these individuals.

For instance, there is a story told of Joe. Joe always saves his last dime when he is on a bender. He goes to the phone, calls the police, and tells them there is a drunk on a certain corner. Then he sits on the curb and waits for the patrol wagon.

There is Frank, the fifty-six-year-old bookkeeper. Frank has been arrested 180 times since 1940. In one recent month he set some sort of record for getting arrested. He was picked up for drunkenness 6 separate times in twenty-seven days.

Then there is "Spike," a retired carpenter who has had 180 arrests since 1935.

Society lacks something when it has no better way of handling the chronic offender than this.

Whose job is Joe? Whose job is Frank? Whose job is Spike?

Are they "jobs" to be left to the officials? To the social worker? To the police officer on the beat? Or to the judge?

Or should every Christian work at these "jobs"?

Dealing with recidivists, of which these folks are extreme examples, constitutes much of the work of courts and jails. It ought to challenge the best social "engineers" in our churches to devise more effective ways of dealing with this discouraging problem.

The experience of the Committee on Institutions has been that two of the most effective ways of preventing the recurrence of crime are probation and parole. However, there is great prejudice in the public mind against both of these procedures. News articles are frequently headlined: "Parolee Kills Man." The Criminal-Court Committee consulted its state department of probation and parole and received some rather startling information which was verified by the National Association of Probation and Parole.

They found that, in the nation as a whole, 85 per cent of the adults placed on probation, instead of being sent to prison, were successful. They lived at home, supported their families, and stayed out of trouble. Only 15 per cent of them were failures. It costs one-tenth as much to supervise an adult on probation as it does to put him in prison.

Of those sent to prison and released on parole before their time was fully served, only 25 per cent failed. The remaining 75 per cent took their proper place in society.

Prisoners who served out their full time returned to the prisons in 60 per cent of the cases. It is believed that if every sentence closed with a period of supervision akin to that of probation this percentage could be reduced.

These facts led the men to conclude that their state could save in men and money by a proper use of probation and parole.

A layman on the Prison Committee found an opportunity to practice his knowledge of probation as one possible alternative to incarceration. He had an employee whose name may be given here as Joe Doremi.

Joe had three children and some unforeseen doctor's bills. He liked to live well like the neighbors. The trouble was that Joe had bought so much on installments (termed the "Budget Plan" to reduce sales resistance) that it took all Joe made to meet living expenses and these payments. What was he to do?

Joe had formerly driven a taxicab and he had taken a lot of people to the race track. An idea! Why not get a real good tip and borrow a little money, go out on his day off, and make enough on a few races to pay his expenses. Joe didn't think of the chance that he might lose. Maybe losers don't ride home in taxicabs.

So Joe went. He borrowed money from friends, and when he came back he was really broke.

No, Joe never intended to be a criminal but he was in a tough spot, and medical bills were due. If Joe could just change some of his delivery tickets from cash to charge, he could keep some of the money he collected for a while and pay it back later. When the company caught up with him, Joe had taken over two hundred dollars, and the appropriation of this much amounts to a felony.

What would you do with Joe?

This is a true story. Society has an answer. It builds a great big house out in the country and calls it the penitentiary, a place for a man to be penitent. However, those who work there say that not all the men are penitent. Yes, society has an answer that removes the man, but what of his wife and children? They are disgraced and without husband or father for a number of years. Mother may get a job and support the children as best she can, but more likely she will go on relief. "This is too bad," says society, "but after all, we can't answer all the problems. Joe should have thought about all that before he committed a felony."

What would you do with Joe? Is there a way to help him? In this case the bonding company paid off. Joe agreed to make restitution and was given a job which did not involve the handling of cash. His employer loaned him some money, and Joe worked out his problem. He was not prosecuted.

Joe's employer spoke to his fellow laymen on the Prison Committee.

"I have an idea that lots of other men like Joe could be saved from prison if we really took seriously the words of the Man who said he came to give deliverance to the captives!"

In talking to the warden the men learned that one county had only one man in the penitentiary—the warden!

"How is this?" they asked.

The warden explained that the usual way of handling the few crimes in his county was by probation rather than imprisonment. Somebody "stood good" for each man who broke the law.

Of course, not all cases are like Joe's. Many cannot be probated, but some can.

Another means of reducing the number of men in prison is by parole. The Prison Committee studied the opinions of penologists on the use of parole. They were told by competent authorities that the chances of many boys for rehabilitation would be greatly improved if they could have some form of supervision when they first came out of prison.

"When you read that a parolee has gone wrong, as some do," the authorities said, "remember that the majority go right. If a man hadn't come out by parole, he would have eventually come out by expiration of his sentence, anyway."

Brown & Bigelow, one of the nation's largest manufacturers of calendars, has given jobs to over three hundred parolees. According to a late report from this firm only four did not justify the confidence placed in them. This outstanding record was not an accident. Charles Ward, company president, made it his business to see that these men made good. There is no substitute for the effect of personal interest in helping a man go straight.

During the depression the prisons of Kentucky, like those of many other states, were terribly overcrowded. Men were sleeping on cots in the corridors. The governor appointed a commission to study the cases, and after study a list of candidates for conditional pardon was prepared. Intensive study was made of the records of these men. Then a good number were given conditional pardons. Whatever public alarm existed over this procedure soon disappeared. There were so few men whose pardons had to be revoked that many people were surprised. This does not prove that all men in prisons should be released, but it does show how the whole problem of probation and parole needs much study by professional and lay people.

This is not a light or a merely sentimental matter. One state with a larger population than Kentucky has a thousand less in its prison. Today a conservative figure on the cost of feeding and housing one prisoner for a year is around a thousand dollars. Multiply this by a thousand and you get a million dollars which Kentucky taxpayers are out of pocket because of this host of unwanted guests!

This does not include the relief costs for prisoners' families and income-tax losses which occur because the men are not earning. But the dollar loss is a small thing compared to the loss of men!

The thing parole boards are concerned about is: *When* should the man come out?—for the fact is that most inmates in our prisons *are* coming out at some time or other. If society really wishes to protect itself from the criminal population, there are only two options: *electrocution or rehabilitation!* The best-known process of rehabilitation is usually a well-handled parole.

The parole board was meeting at a state reformatory. The first man to be considered was a redheaded boy in his early twenties. Despite his youth he had a discouraging record. Like many boys in prison he had come from a broken home. He had been in two homes for delinquent boys, then in two prisons—altogether in four correctional institutions. He had violated two felony paroles. With a record like that his chances to be given another parole were poor.

But on that parole board was a man who in World War II had lost his only child—a redheaded boy. Despite warnings from colleagues he offered to take the boy as his responsibility.

Then came the effort. Every Sunday, and sometimes during the week, the man visited that boy. For eight months there was uncertainty. Then, gradually, the boy came to see life in a different light. He decided that the *right way* was the *best way* to live. The man kept up his interest—continued to visit the boy—and the boy held steadfast to his resolution to become a productive citizen. A different expression showed on his face. He realized that he had been the one who was out of step. In time the law released its hold on him and from last accounts he continues to do well and justifies the confidence his sponsor placed in him.

What are the ideas of the man who did this big job?

It doesn't do a bit of good to tell the boy you are interested in society or in humanity. He needs to know that you really care about him. Unless he can believe that, his disillusionment may continue. He will feel as so many in prison do: that he is rejected, guilty, and that every man's hand is against him. When a boy feels that every man's hand is against him, it is only natural that he should be against every man. That's what people call antisocial.

It seemed to the Prison Committee that Christian laymen ought to know their parole-board members better and learn some of the things they have learned. The practice of taking redheaded boys for supervision ought to be increased. Well, maybe it's not just a question of the color of the hair.

The following letter was written to his son by a committeeman who has given considerable time and thought to the rehabilitation of men returning from correctional institutions.

Dear Son:

I wish a lot of people could have been with me as I took Jim Brown from Woodfield Reformatory yesterday afternoon. He came to the office at a little after twelve noon. Mr. Jones, a former staff member there, brought him and recommended him highly—the man "he'd feel free to take in his own home." "We don't get too many like him out there." This checks with other reports that I have on him.

He was well-dressed, but his wardrobe was meager—he had it all on! He had no overcoat, but I had one waiting. I took him to lunch. He was nervous—"stunned," as he put it. It had been two years since he ate with a knife and fork.

Going home, I found an old suitcase; I put in a towel, a washcloth, razor and soap, socks and garters, pajamas, shorts and vest, paper and envelopes, pen and pencil. Surprising how things go in pairs, isn't it?

Mother went with me as I took him down to Maple and Fourth, which was close to his rooming house. I telephoned Dr. Williams, the pastor of the nearest church of his denomination, told Jim I had done so, and steered him that way. I plan to see Jim tomorrow.

I talked with him about his new job. He looks too good to be true, but I am not forgetting that he has served more than one term and may be a bad risk. We will work on him. Any suggestions?

It does seem to me that if every boy coming out had a man to meet him and follow up, we'd have less recidivism. Well, this is an interesting experiment. Why will people spend time and money on a horse or dog when the same time and money can assist the development of a man?

Love,
Dad

To be very realistic about it, this "Dad" had his hopes for the parolee disappointed. The forger started drinking and forged again. Not all cases work out well. But this failure did not shatter Dad's faith in the possibilities of working with such men. Jesus said, "I was in prison, and ye came unto me."

6

A Job with a Future

Any man worth his salt wants to know the future possibilities of his job. Is there room for advancement? Are there problems yet to be solved? Can he help discover better ways of doing the work?

When the Committee on Institutions faced the needs of child-care agencies in its town, it discovered a job with future possibilities unlimited. The intriguing thing about work with children is that all sorts of latent powers lie in their personalities, waiting to be called forth by the right influence.

If one were to seek the name of the greatest man of secular history, allowing all centuries and countries to set forth their choicest, allowing all walks of life to be considered, one name that would likely stand supreme would be that of Aristotle. Living over 2,300 years ago, Aristotle is credited with having done more than any other to influence the course of human thinking and to set up the categories of knowledge which are the foundation of science. He trained the man who conquered the world of his day—Alexandria of Macedonia.

Yet when Aristotle was very young, his father and mother both died, and he went to the home of (Mr. and Mrs.) Proxenus. This fact seems unusually important when we learn that the goal in child care today is to provide for children in foster homes, using institutional care only in temporary emergencies. The story of Aristotle thus speaks volumes for the opportunity of the foster parent. Perhaps you can suggest some modern Proxenus to the child-placement worker in your community.

Later Aristotle went to "college" in Athens under the great teacher Plato. Could you suggest some school like that of Plato's for a twentieth-century Aristotle? Would you suggest your old college? What was it that the Greeks did for this orphaned boy that we could do today?

In a little mission Sunday school a small boy seemed bent on doing all the mean tricks a small boy can devise. He pinched; he pulled hair. He pulled chairs from under people about to sit down. He seemed to be obsessed with the idea of making everyone unhappy. In short, he was the personification of an imp.

"Despite that youngster's general reputation and specific conduct," a wise woman present said, "something is making that boy act like that." And she questioned his mother. What do you suppose she learned? It was his birthday. He did not have the pennies, one for each year, to put in the birthday box. He felt embarrassed, inferior, and unloved.

The wise woman got the necessary pennies and gave them to the boy's mother. And the mother gave them to the boy. Lo, the imp became an angel—for the rest of the Sunday-school session, at any rate. He is grown now, and his impish tendencies have never got him into trouble. Perhaps it is because that woman kept up an interest in him.

However, some of our boys and girls are not so fortunate. They have no wise woman or man who will provide the necessary guidance. Lacking help in the use of the large amount of spare time which child-labor laws have provided, these boys and girls often release their abundant energies into socially destructive channels.

In one city within a few months juveniles made vandalous assaults on a public library, two cemeteries, two churches, and a woman's club.

At the library, phonograph records were smashed, cards and books torn and scattered. At the cemetery, monuments were overturned and broken. The damage there alone ran into thousands of dollars. In the churches the altars were desecrated. In the woman's club, upholstery was ripped, water left running, and pictures were destroyed.

When incidents like these are commonplace, there is something drastically wrong with our way of rearing children or with our way of life as a whole. In the face of a rising juvenile-delinquency rate the layman as well as the policeman, judge, and social worker is responsible for finding ways to do something about it. There is little doubt that the problem is complex, but its complexity is no excuse for inactivity. Something can, something *must* be done, and done by the layman. Neither the professional social worker nor the law-enforcement officer can do it all. In most cases there are things that can be done in juvenile courts, in children's homes, and in the community itself.

For example, it would be interesting to study the effect of restoring to young people their right to work, with proper safeguards. Many people are beginning to feel that denying youth the opportunity to work contributes to the growth of the attitude that they "don't count," and that "the world owes me a living." Perhaps if mama were to stay home and let Johnny help earn, it might do some good on the American scene.

The following letter, which appeared in the Louisville *Courier-Journal* (July 6, 1948), tells how one community took some action on this approach to the problem.

To the Editor:

Gradually it is dawning upon the minds of the good people of this country that amusement and play are not the final cure for juvenile delinquency. The remedy is work.

In the 18th and early 19th centuries it was possible to rear large families of children, because, beginning at about 7 years of age, boys and girls were able to work around the home and on the farm, so that they were no longer a burden to their parents. At 14 boys were apprenticed, and their employers supported them. At 21 they were qualified journeymen, ready to support themselves and start their own families. Today most children are dependent until they are at least 18 years old. If they go to college, the support must continue until they are 22 or 23 years old. This is a great burden on their parents and on the community and is economically wrong.

The Board of Education of New York City has done some constructive work in order to remedy this evil, in what they call their Co-operative Education for High School Pupils. One boy or girl goes to school for a week, while an alternating boy or girl is employed in business. The next week they exchange places; the one in school goes to business and the one in business goes to school.

Miss Grace Brennan, in charge of this department, says that during the fiscal year ending June 1947, 3,000 school children took advantage of this system and earned a total of over $90,000 in wages. That amount of money would be a considerable help in their support.

Many existing laws stand in the way of useful employment of minors, laws supposedly for the benefit of children, but actually a great hardship to them.

The young people would be much happier and less inclined to get into mischief if they had congenial employment with a reasonable amount of responsibility and adequate compensation. When both the parents and the public realize this and work together to bring about such reform juvenile delinquency will be on the decline.
Glen Ridge, N.J.

James Emery Brooks [1]

One layman of the Juvenile-Court Committee surveyed sixteen educators, principals, and superintendents of schools on the question: "In your opinion are the child-labor laws a major contributing factor to juvenile delinquency?" Thirteen of the sixteen said, "Yes."

The Juvenile-Court Committee took as a project the enlistment of qualified laymen from their churches to serve as sponsors for boys and girls probated by the court. They worked closely with the judge and social worker. The sponsors were coached through the use of a manual called the *Youth Sponsorship Guide.*

A real encouragement came to these sponsors when the committee received the following letter from two boys, ages fourteen and sixteen. This letter gives a "delinquent's-eye view" of the sponsorship plan and of the work of the Juvenile-Court Committee:

[1] Used by permission of the Louisville *Courier-Journal* and Mrs. Eleanor Brooks de Vore.

1/11/55

Dear Sir:

We would like to tell you how much we appreciate. The break you have given us. And we sure have learn our lesson not to mix with the wrong people. Mr. Cline has really been nice to us. When he talks to us like a real friend. We have been keeping out of trouble for all this time, and we know that we can do it for the rest of the time.

Yours Truly,

Names Withheld

Orphanages, any groups of homeless children, make a tremendous appeal to big-hearted men. They will dig down into their jeans, or they will perform lots of tasks like running a booth or selling tickets. Yet if your boy or mine were in an institution, we would feel that this was good but not entirely adequate. Somebody would have to think with imagination. Something would have to be done for heart hungers and the need for understanding. Heart hungers and the need for understanding are more difficult to satisfy than bodily hungers and the need for clothing. They are things money can't buy.

A boy from the children's home was caught with goods he had stolen from a store when on a visit to town. Needless to say, the goods were returned. But someone at the home overheard other boys talking about the incident. Their attitude was that the boy had had tough luck in being caught.

Someone has to change such attitudes. The Council of Churchwomen was asked to appoint a committee to study the children's home. This was to be an experiment, but it worked well. Women can do many things for a children's home that men might never think of or be able to do. Some women's groups were already interested in this home. One local church had found a big sister for every Protestant girl in this home.

"If my daughter were in such a home," said a layman who heard of this plan, "I would rather something like that were done for her than almost anything I can think of."

The men's committee wants to find a big brother for each boy.

At Christmas one generous luncheon club gives a big party for the children's home. Children are asked in advance what they want. One boy asked for a wrist watch. He received it. After a few days he pried off the back and took out the works, played with them, then threw them away. He stretched the metal wristband across the room and threw it away. Asked why he did this, he said, "I wanted to see what makes it tick. I didn't care for it." That boy needs a big brother to show him the value of property, of gratitude, of appreciation. Such a person would render him an infinitely greater service than the man who generously gave him a wrist watch—as fine as was the impulse that caused the gift.

There are other things men's groups can do. A scout troop can be organized if the home does not have one. Children may be invited on outings, especially visits to the home of the big brother or big sister. Children may be taken to town for dental or medical appointments. One summer the ladies of the committee provided transportation to a vacation Bible school for each child who wanted to attend. The committee needs to be well acquainted with the staff of the home so that they may give intelligent support and assistance. Managing a child-care institution is a big job.

Key laymen should know the superintendent. They should also get acquainted with the social worker. The latter lays down the pattern involved in their co-operation. The social worker in the institution is like the doctor in the hospital: as he prescribes for the patients in the hospital, so she prescribes for the youngsters. It is just as bad to overlook the social worker as it is to leave the entire job up to her. She carries a heavy case load and usually welcomes any help in taking care of "her" children.

A prominent writer took her granddaughter riding shortly before Christmas. They passed an orphanage and the little girl wanted to go in and play with the children. The grandmother did as grandmothers are said sometimes to do—she granted the child's desire. The little girl had a delightful time playing. When she returned to the automobile, her grandmother asked if she would like to give these children something for Christmas. The child thought that would be fine.

"What would you like to give them?" asked the grandmother. "What do you suppose they would rather have than anything else in the world?"

The child's face grew serious. She thought for a moment and then said, "I know, a mama and a papa!"

Children in institutions do not have a mama and a papa, though the cottage mother and father are often wonderful people and do their best to try to be just that. Incidentally, in a children's home near Louisville the superintendent is gradually placing young, dedicated couples in charge of the cottages as the older housemothers have to be replaced.

Taking care of children is a big job. It taxes the best ability of the best mothers. Taking care of other people's children is a big and difficult job. Taking care of twelve to twenty-five children with the background and problems such as one finds in a children's home is a job that should get all the support, assistance, and encouragement that the public, especially church people, can give.

In Frankfort, Kentucky, there is an area known as the "Corner of Celebrities." It is so-called because from it there came in one generation ten nationally famous men. Among them were an admiral, an ambassador, two United States senators, and a Supreme Court justice.

There has been considerable conjecture as to how this happened. Was there some personality who gave these boys a vision and caused them to continue to aspire after other boys had leveled off? Could it have been some minister or schoolteacher?

How wonderful it would be if we could discover the plan for producing great men and then include this plan in the working of our child-care institutions. Since defective homes are said to be the cause of most crimes, if we could cause children's homes to be the opposite of the defective homes, wouldn't it be really wonderful?

This is a serious job—an important job—a job with a future. The rearing of a greater generation is the greatest business of this generation. It is for the children of today that we build everything—not only schools, but roads and railroads, bridges and factories, stores, skyscrapers, and churches. For whom but the children, the men and women who are to be, do men do all their great work?

Two men were touring the area of Lincoln's boyhood. One was a prominent church and civic leader who had made many speeches about Abraham Lincoln. When they came to the place where Abraham Lincoln had spent a considerable part of his boyhood, he said with much feeling, "This is the place which produced Abraham Lincoln."

The other man said, "Do you think the shape of those hills, the curve of that stream, and the way the road runs had anything to do with the personality of Abraham Lincoln?"

"Why not?"

"Well, if I believed that, I would resign my job tomorrow and build an orphanage here and raise Abraham Lincolns wholesale!"

We do not know how to raise Abraham Lincolns wholesale, but we do know something about the ways to give a child love and friendship. Working with children of the juvenile court and of the children's homes is a job with a future.

7

Working with
the Great Physician

A committee of interested laymen decided to visit the emergency ward of the general hospital late one Saturday night. There injured persons were being given initial treatment. The victims of the automobile crash, the cut, bruised, and intoxicated "bum," the fellow with a knife wound from the cafe fight—all were there that night.

The inspiring thing was not the picture of suffering but the picture of service. There were some people serving as volunteers, having taken training in order to be qualified to help. In an unheralded sort of way they were rendering quiet though strenuous service to a hospital which is always limited in funds, but which has a tremendous job to do with the dollars it gets.

The Committee on Institutions asked a group of men from four large downtown churches to study the work of the city-supported general hospital. The size of the institution with its emergency ward, psychiatric ward, surgical and medical wards and clinics was impressive. It was difficult to know where to start in any attempt to help.

First, the committee sought out the hospital administrator and told him of its friendly interest. It made clear that it was not conducting "an investigation." In one of the committee meetings the men discussed study topics and the administrator was able to make some suggestions. As the discussion moved along, the following questions were raised:

1. What are the various causes of people being here?
2. What average, maximum, and minimum time do people spend here.
3. What are the ages of the inmates?
4. What does it cost per day per patient?
5. What are the religious preferences of people in the institution? What service is being rendered by the denominations—Catholic, Methodist, Baptist, Jew?
6. What food, what medical and dental care, what recreational, educational, and religious services are provided?
7. What is done for the personality of people here? What rehabilitation, what integration?
8. What are the trends in this institution's field?
9. How do institutions of this kind operate in other cities, in other countries?
10. Has this institution been rated by a national agency? In what respects does it excel? In what respects does it lack?
11. What have others done successfully to reduce the need of people to come here?
12. What other community agencies are working in this field? How can we co-operate with these agencies?

As the men "peeled off" and each took some one of the special questions to study and report on, they spotted certain obvious needs.

To begin with, they were convinced that the public institution is not the place for proselyting, and even evangelizing has to be carried on with restraint and tact. Plenty of people outside need evangelizing, but the sick patient is not fair game for the impetuous. The experienced and skilled minister will verify this.

The committeemen learned, however, that there was no system of *notifying the pastors* of people who came into the hospital as patients. Feeling that it would be a good thing for the minister and for the patient, they arranged to get some information about the person's religious connections taken at the time of admission. Then they provided cards that could be mailed to the patient's pastor.

Since city and county hospitals must give primacy to medical and nursing care in operating on their limited budgets, the religious care of such patients often falls to such volunteer help as is interested. Religious ministry to patients is tied in closely with the question of *personal visiting.* Too much visiting is not good, but the committee discovered that many people in this hospital never had visitors. It discovered that if it sought some training in visiting and mastered some simple rules such as: "Ask the nurse first," "Listen rather than talk," "Don't try to put over any views," it could make a real contribution to the morale of the patients. After a period of visiting it began to feel that this was not an adequate ministry for such a large institution. It felt that a chaplain was needed to provide supervision for the over-all religious needs of the hospital.

Suppose you are lying in one of these beds. You are very sick. Other people in the ward have had visitors, but you have had none. You are alone, very much alone and afraid. Then the hospital chaplain comes in. He comes to visit you. He is friendly, understanding, and helpful. He comes back again. You find that there is someone who cares, after all. You have a friend. Don't you think you'd have a new appreciation for Matt. 25:36: "I was sick, and ye visited me"?

Having a real friend at a time like that has a lot to do with the speed of recovery.

What could the committee do to help the hospital secure a minister who could do such work?

The committee began to study the matter of religious ministry in hospitals. It learned that an increasing number of private hospitals, many of which are sponsored by various Christian bodies, are adding clinically trained chaplains to their staffs. In fact, the demand for such ministers far exceeds the supply. But the private hospital usually has some sort of constituency which is concerned for its needs.

"What about our city and county hospital?" the committee asked. "Who will see to it that their patients have the benefit of adequate spiritual care?"

The conviction began to grip it that this was its job—its work in assisting the great Physician. A member of the committee knew that at a nearby theological seminary there was a program for the clinical training of ministers. Such training prepared them for the sort of work the hospital seemed to need. The professor in charge of this work was asked to recommend someone if means could be found to employ him. After referring the matter to the larger organization, the city church council, the committee worked out a plan for the employment of a graduate student from the seminary as part-time chaplain.

"If my wife or son or daughter were in the hospital,

I'd be mighty glad there was a trained minister at hand," said one committeeman. "And I have found that this chaplain knows how to listen, as well as talk. Why, he even has a lot of downright horse sense."

The hospital chaplain, whose services are sponsored by the Council of Churches, works closely with the hospital visitors from the committee and other groups. He conducts services and counsels with the Protestant patients. One indication of the success of this program is that the chaplaincy is now a full-time position and the chaplain is helping to train other seminary students in hospital work.

In addition to the general-hospital group the Committee on Institutions includes a group which does similar work at the nearby state mental hospital.

The treatment of some forms of mental disease often requires considerable periods of time, just as the treatment of tuberculosis does. This fact, in addition to the shortage of private facilities and psychiatrists, has placed a tremendous and ever-increasing burden on the state. It is not unusual, therefore, to find two thousand patients in a state mental hospital even where the state supports more than one such institution.

Great strides have been made in the effectiveness of our state hospitals in recent years. More and more treatment is being given. The mental-hygiene movement has done much to create public sentiment in favor of better support for these hospitals. Buildings must be maintained, competent personnel must be found and trained, and the patients must be clothed, fed, and, if possible, helped to recover. The task of administering a mental hospital is tremendous, yet for the most part it must be done on a minimal budget.

The men of the Mental-Hospital Committee encouraged the hospital in its plans to use more volunteer help, which is one way, though not an easy one, around the personnel cost problem. The hospital recently employed a director of volunteer service to coordinate and train the helpers from church and civic groups in visiting, entertaining, and serving the patients.

Problems confronting the head of such an institution are numerous and varied. As the administrator shares his problems with the committee, its members become better acquainted not only with the specific needs of the establishment but also the general field in which it operates. This increases the effectiveness of their service.

At the state hospital the committee helped the hospital secure a clinically trained chaplain. It sponsored an annual recognition dinner for the staff personnel, to show its appreciation. It collected reading material. It tried to find ways to break the sense of *aloneness* which the patient often feels. Special remembrances of Christmas and birthdays helped greatly. Articles the patient is likely to need, such as toothpaste, a comb, stationery, and fruit were individually packed in "Sunshine Bag" as another morale lifter.

The same problem of loneliness was found by the committee which took the state tuberculosis sanatorium as its special responsibility. Here it found the patients were all from outside the county. The county provided its own hospital. These people were all a long way from home. At the request of the administrator the committee went to work. It organized the hospital library, provided hymnbooks for religious services, set up a visitation program, and in general helped dispel the cloud of isolation in which many of the patients felt they were enveloped.

When the city set up a new hospital to care for the chronically ill, a committee was on hand to help. In one of the first meetings the administrator and several staff members were asked by the laymen to suggest some of their needs.

"I know one thing we need," said the occupational therapist. "Newspapers! We have only one paper for 150 patients. You should hear some of them complain about not getting it. They want to keep up with the world."

One of the laymen asked, "How many copies do you think would be adequate?"

The therapist thought a moment. "If we had one for each hall, that would be six. Would that be too many?"

The next morning, and every morning since, six copies of the paper have been delivered to the hospital, with the compliments of the neighboring churches. One layman with determination was the key.

The committee for this hospital also sponsors a series of religious services and a visitation program.

There *are* ways for churchmen to take up jobs with the great Physician.

8

Men Wanted

Lately there has been quite an upswing of the idea that every child of God should have a job in his kingdom. One minister puts it this way: "Ingrowing religion isn't enough." A theological-seminary professor says: "Church people have more to do than listen to a good man talk." Elton Trueblood's book *Your Other Vocation* and Wilbur La Roe, Jr.'s, *The Church We Love* have had wide acceptance. The Christophers, Inc. movement, led by Father James Keller, has attracted many. The Christophers theme, "You Can Change the World," challenges the individual to light a candle rather than curse the darkness. Through this movement many persons are being led to find work in the fields that influence the masses of people: government, education, literature, entertainment. There they attempt to use their influence in a constructive way.

The assumption of the Committee on Institutions has been that every individual who joins a church ought to "join" some responsibility. His accepted tasks should include not only those within the organization of his church but outreaching jobs as well. Jesus didn't say, "Ye are the salt of the *church*," but "Ye are the salt of the *earth*."

There is quite a lot of concern among thinking men

over the fact that Americans are becoming so largely a nation of spectators. When we put in our forty hours, we want to relax and watch somebody else play ball. Men aplenty have been saying that there ought to be some way of harnessing the resources within the church to the needs of the community.

Horses, men, and motors have power, but the power is not of much value unless it is harnessed to some task.

The person who started the gag that preachers are paid to be good, but laymen are good for nothing, stated an idea that many people actually have. Institutional work is only a small sector of what should be attempted. Congregations have more to do than congregate. Laymen have more to do than pass the plate on Sunday and pass the buck on Monday. Each man needs a "magnificent obsession."

The plain fact is that too many of us are like the men described by Jesus in his parable of the laborers and the vineyard (Matt. 20:1-16). The owner went to the market place at the eleventh hour and asked those there, "Why stand ye here all the day idle?"

Their excuse was, "Because no man hath hired us."

The owner then said, "Go ye also into the vineyard."

Men are still idle today. How can they be effectively hired for labor in the Lord's vineyard? What is the secret of effective lay enlistment?

A salesman's formula is: Attention—interest—desire —action.

A social worker's formula is: Rapport—planning, explanation—acceptance.

A schoolteacher's formula is: Preparation of the pupil's mind—transition—illustration—repetition.

Is there a similar formula for enlisting men in practical service?

Talking to Homer Carpenter, for over twenty-five years pastor of Louisville's First Christian Church, the chairman of the Committee on Institutions asked, "How do you enlist men?" Dr. Carpenter's church seemed to furnish an unusual number of leaders for civic enterprises.

"Keep the conditions right," was the pastor's reply. He illustrated this by describing a brilliant flower garden on Mackinac Island where the natural conditions were just right for growing flowers.

Perhaps it is not such a simple matter as using a formula mechanically. Many people feel about methods like one of the great ball players who was asked to name the seven ways of sliding to base. When he had promptly listed them, he was asked which one of them he used. "I don't know," he replied; "I just slide."

Methods may get in the way of some people's operation, but generally it is well to pay some attention to the methods that have grown out of tested experience. Fifteen years' experience has taught the Committee on Institutions some of these methods for mobilizing man power.

"It is about as hard to get one of these groups organized and keep it going," says the chairman, "as it is to start and maintain a men's Bible class."

To anyone who should ask their method of enlistment the committee would first say: *Pick your man.* Jesus never called for volunteers. Nowhere in the New Testament does Jesus say, "Every man who will do this, hold up his hand." Jesus picked his men, and he knew whom he was calling. Although the committee has no formal testing or screening devices, it does seek out men that it feels have something worth while to share—some skill or talent, some attitude or outlook. Pick your man with considerable care.

Another feature of the committee's approach to recruitment is the idea: *Enlist men for specific tasks.* Men are much more likely to do when they are clear on what is to be done. There is a place here for the marvelous diversity of personalities and special skills which we find in even the smallest community.

Can we not use a theoretical man who seeks truth? An economic man who seeks results? An aesthetic man who seeks the fitness of things. A political man who seeks leadership? A social man who loves his fellow man? A religious man who seeks the highest good? Cannot all these contribute in finding out how to discover the main problems of our time? Can they not together show us how the attempt to deal with some of these problems may provide a way to become doers of the word and not hearers only? Do we not need to enlist the keenest men within our various church communions to study such problems?

Operating on the basis of a belief that men could be challenged to give time and effort to a practical service project, the committee has developed various offices to make it easy to enlist a man at the point of his interest.

They found the following offices to be helpful in defining responsibility:

A *chairman,* assisted by a steering committee, to plan meetings, discuss objectives, contact similar interest groups

A *secretary* to keep minutes, send notices of meetings, promote public interest

A *treasurer* to collect funds and manage the financial business of the committee

A *personnel man* to enlist capable men who can perform special tasks on the committee

A *contact man* to inform the committee about what other groups, such as clubs, are doing in the field

An *information man* to present to the committee clippings from magazines and books pertaining to their work

A *fiscal man* to study the financial setup of the institution

A *publicity man* to get the story of the institution over to the public, using the superintendent and staff on radio, television, and before Bible classes and clubs

Remarkable response has been received when high-grade men are asked to do specific tasks. Maybe this is due to the fact that the men are asked to do something that they know they are particularly able to do. For the problem of an institutional farm they got a retired farmer. When there was a problem of an institutional newspaper, they got a newspaper man. A problem in education called for a professor from a local university.

Of course, all these tasks had been requested by the institution head. He was delighted to have men from the committee help him because he knew their rule, "We will make no unfavorable public criticism of the management of any institution we study and seek to serve." As far as is known there has been no violation of any confidence received by the committee in its fifteen years of operation. Such a reputation is a great asset.

In enlisting a specific man, remember the techniques

of the salesman whose program is built around the idea of favorable attention, interest, desire, and action.

Suppose you were going to undertake to get a man interested in the plight of a prisoner discharged from jail or a prison, especially one with no job, no resources, no friends, and with a knowledge of crime just sharpened by a refresher course in the great schools of crime maintained at such expense by the state. Calling a big building a penitentiary does not make men penitent; calling it a reformatory does not make men reform. Here is this man turned loose! Suppose you were in his place and couldn't get a job and knew how to break in houses or write bad checks. When you get to thinking about it, you want to do something; you may want to reform our prison system. We ought to have some substitute for a prison. Certainly we ought to make more use of probation which has done such good work where it has been given good personnel.

Problems of this kind are not handled quickly. But if we study them, we can do something significant. Many stories are told of men who achieved by studying and staying with a specific problem. There are lots of things you can do when you try. The response received when men are asked to take a probated or even a paroled convict for counseling, or when the juvenile court asks for counselors for some boys, shows men can be appealed to for this work.

Attention, interest, desire, action—these are not too hard to get if you have picked your man and defined the problem.

The factor upon which enlistment is maintained is *the building of enthusiasm*. Enthusiasm comes by paying attention to details. Look at a snowflake under a microscope and it becomes a miracle of geometric design—a masterpiece of miraculously measured and matched numbers. Or listen to any ball fan: he knows the fine points of the game. Study the problem and you become enthusiastic about the need being met and you may communicate that enthusiasm to others.

One of the best ways to stimulate interest is through a personal visit to the institution, many of which we have described earlier in the story.

Well-run committee meetings are also interest builders. Each of the institutional committees, the Jail, Prison, Police-Court Committees, and the rest meet monthly. Although the usual procedure of beginning with prayer and reading the minutes and subcommittee reports is followed, a rigid schedule in meetings is avoided at all cost. Formalities are kept at a minimum. Friendliness is the keynote. Initiative and creative thought are the main objectives.

From time to time speakers are brought in, but they are usually men who are on the staff of the agency being studied. They open up problem areas for discussion. Sometimes committeemen prepare papers on their own relating to a need or problem area facing their institutions.

One man who had belonged to several conversation clubs found participation in them very stimulating. Each member presented some topic for discussion once a year or so. Then there was a period of "round-the-circle" discussion in which each member was asked to give in three minutes his ideas on the subject being presented.

"How come," said this man, "there could not be such a thing as a church conversation club? Why couldn't we use this pattern for our meetings and get the benefit of everyone's ideas as to what could be done in a given situation?"

The stories in preceding chapters give numerous examples of how insights emerge in such meetings where the "conversation club" plan is followed.

Yes, the fields are white with possibilities for service, but the age-old question is, "Where are the laborers?" Have we really organized in this area? In our churches we have organized for purposes of evangelism, stewardship, education, and pastoral care. It is now time to organize for the purpose of making men useful. In this task every member becomes a minister, and the clergyman becomes a coach.

Men Wanted!

9

Difficulties and Hazards

It would be strange indeed if the story of these committees was entirely one of successes. There have been setbacks. There have been times when the going was tediously slow. The first committee faced this prospect in the beginning when it chose to plan a long pull with the hope for lasting gain rather than planning a reform wave with the possibility of speedy decline.

Some of the difficulties of the committee work are named here lest the reader assume that these men have received a special grace making failure impossible for them. Most of the weaknesses of the program are those familiar to Sunday-school and civic-club members.

For example, there is the basic problem of *enlistment*, the methodology of which was discussed in the preceding chapter. The committee always needs more men. Bill Smith's company transfers him to another city just as he is getting into the swing of things. Warren Craig's law practice begins to require so much time that some of his committee work has to give. A college dean who has an important subcommittee chairmanship and is a top resource person is sent abroad as adviser to a foreign government. And so it goes.

To meet the continuing need for enlistment many of the committees make one member the personnel man. His job is to recruit new members from the churches which make up the committee. This calls for close co-operation with the pastors and leaders of the neighboring churches. The personnel man may call or visit the members to build attendance at the meetings. In this phase of his work he has the help of the office staff of the local Council of Churches. Minutes of meetings are filed in the office and mailed to members. Announcements of meetings usually go out about a week in advance.

Attendance and enlistment are improved when each man has a specific task. Office records are a help here, in that an assignment and planning sheet is kept for each committee showing what these jobs are. The current assignment sheet of the Prison Committee shows North is the chairman. Green is a contact man to keep the committee informed about the work of allied groups at the prison. West is responsible for showing a religious film each third week. Black is chairman of the subcommittee which studies the operation of the institutional farm. Jones is working on plans for improving parole procedure. Gray is studying the possibilities of creating a concrete-products industry. White is sponsoring a special Dale Carnegie course for inmates. Doe is studying the prison's educational program. Another is studying the religious activities. Two others are sponsoring a self-help group among the inmates.

When the roster of members is kept fresh and up-to-date, when attendance is regular, when assignments are made and accepted, the operation of this and other committees in the setup proceeds smoothly. Something for every man to work on, a definite project for each church represented on the committee—that puts the entire undertaking in proper focus.

The easy part of the job is to get these assignments down on paper. Encouraging the men to stick at them and to get results is more difficult. This is where the idea that the layman is a minister and the clergyman a coach fits in. Coaching the men is a primary task of the committee chairmen and secretaries.

A second problem with which the committees have to deal is the matter of *orientation*. Committee policy of no public criticism is so strange to most new members that it usually takes some little while for the new attitudes to sink in. Occasionally committee leadership finds itself a bit afield. When this happens it proves helpful to return to the principles on which the Committee on Institutions was founded years ago. These basic ideas help keep new and old "workers" on the main line. Not that there is a closed system and only one way to get things done. On the contrary. Many of the committees that have had the most success have been among the most unorthodox. But until some better and more workable plan is devised, it is suggested to committees that they follow what experience has shown to be a generally helpful approach:

1. No unfavorable public criticism
2. Awareness of some community need
3. Support of good institutional management
4. Service to patients and inmates
5. Prevention of the need for the institution
6. A job for every member
7. Round-the-circle discussion
8. No canned programs

Most of these principles have been illustrated earlier in the book, but perhaps a further word is in order here about the second item mentioned above: creating an awareness that a need exists. For example, in Louisville, a city known for its horse racing, the criminal-court group became concerned about the influx of professional gamblers. Court officials showed them how gambling breeds crime and undermines the law-enforcement agency itself. Instead of yelling louder for more enforcement, the committee decided to launch an educational venture.

It wanted to create a public awareness of the gambling problem. It wanted people to be able to distinguish legitimate business risk from gambling. In a legitimate business risk if one person gains, others gain; in a gambling risk, if one person wins, somebody loses. Gambling is poor sportsmanship. It is really making money out of another's loss, profiting from poverty.

In order to get this message across, the committee prepared a small booklet called *Gambling in a Nutshell*. They found a cartoonist who illustrated the simple and pointed text with pungent sketches. The booklet traced the degrading effect of gambling on the moral life. It showed that the infiltration of gamblers into a community is followed shortly by the demoralization of the officers of the law.

Thousands of copies of the booklet were distributed. A special effort was made to place it in the hands of high-school young people. So many requests were received for it from other cities that it became necessary to reprint it.

Improvements in community life wait upon the constructive molding of community opinion. Christian forces have a real challenge to help create a healthy awareness of community needs. This has to precede any permanent answer to those needs.

A third difficulty the committees have encountered is the matter of *continuity*. When a committee is working well, the members are taking initiative. There is a good deal of freedom in matters of opinion and action. When meetings are creative and stimulating, many good ideas are brought to the surface. If allowed to pass without notice, their value is lost. The continuity of the committee's work is broken, and later work cannot benefit from previous thought and study. In order to conserve these ideas and suggestions, the committee keeps another form of record called an "Idea Sheet." In this way the committee has a kind of reservoir of projects for possible consideration. Good ideas are not as likely to get lost. Continuity of effort is assured.

Take the Prison Committee, for example. The following tentative plans made up the idea sheet for this group a short while ago. Since then some positive action has been taken on all of these items.

1. See what assistance the committee can be to the Society for Personality Adjustment and Development of Education (a self-help group for the inmates).

2. Investigate the possibility of the committee sponsoring the Dale Carnegie course for inmates. It has been used in other prisons.

3. Provide a regular Tuesday-night community sing and lecture series.

4. Promote handicraft among the inmates as a means of earning money to help support their families.

5. Conduct a program of legislative research in the matter of parole. What changes would increase the rehabilitative

possibilities of parole? What is a better answer to the problem of delinquency than prisons?

6. Furnish a regular Thursday-night program of movies, including some religious films.

7. Investigate the possibility of securing a prison farm.

8. Be of service to the program of the chaplain.

Sometimes it is discouraging when ideas which have been listed on the sheet for long periods of time seem to lie dormant. It may be because the right man has not been given a vision of what could be done. Again, it may be because some outward circumstance of local government is unfavorable toward the change we seek. Large amounts of patience, persistence, and tact are required to nurture these seedling ideas into the age of fruit bearing. Some are quite hardy and press on to maturity. Some are slow growers. And, of course, some are weak and die before maturity.

For folks who believe that religion is more than warming a bench on Sunday there are bound to be difficulties and hazards—but also opportunities. We have tried to tell here some ways that lawyers, teachers, engineers, printers, farmers, restaurant men, and factory workers in Louisville have found to give hands and feet to the Christian message.

What they have done *you* can do in your town—do it in your own way, but do!

Why not get started?

Too long we have been conditioned to hear somebody talk, and then go home and forget about it. We build expensive edifices, install costly organs, engage trained choirs, and properly put great emphasis on great messages from the pulpit. In many churches we have nurseries for wee youngsters and coffee and doughnuts for weak oldsters. But we have not been conditioned in our Christian life to take a problem and think it through, to keep working on it, to keep asking, "What would the Master do about this; what would he want me to do about it?"

"I was sick. . . ."

"I was in prison. . . ."

Are you going to do anything about it?

APPENDIX

National Agencies

It is sometimes desirable to know how well the job is being done at a particular institution. People are inclined to be guided by casual impressions, newspaper stories, and legislative investigations. All these may have their value, but there is another way.

The staffs of national organizations such as those listed below are not only technically equipped and well informed in the field but have a sympathetic, constructive, and helpful approach to the problems of an institution. The costs for such services are sometimes surprisingly low.

The best-intentioned of amateurs may make excellent observations and criticisms of the work of the institutions. On the other hand, he not only may miss the most vital features; he may be shocked by something that may not be bad. The right way to evaluate any institution is to have it done by men whose judgment is based upon years of specialized experience. Experts are available. We amateurs are not sufficiently equipped to evaluate any institution. We may strain at a gnat and swallow a camel. Among the good national agencies are:

PENAL

American Correctional Association
E. R. Cass, General Secretary
135 East 15th Street
New York 3, N.Y.

Bureau of Prisons
James V. Bennett, Director
U.S. Department of Justice
Washington 25, D.C.

National Jail Association
Frank F. Kenton, Executive Secretary
427 West Street
New York 14, N.Y.

National Probation and Parole Association
Will C. Turnbladh, Executive Director
1790 Broadway
New York 19, N.Y.

CHILD CARE

Boys' Clubs of America, Inc.
David W. Armstrong, Executive Director
381 Fourth Avenue
New York 16, N.Y.

Child Welfare League of America, Inc.
Joseph H. Reid, Executive Director
345 East 46th Street
New York 17, N.Y.

Children's Bureau
Martha M. Eliot, Chief
U.S. Department of Health, Education and Welfare
Washington 25, D.C.

HEALTH

American Hospital Association
Dr. Edwin L. Crosby, Director
18 East Division Street
Chicago 10, Illinois

American Protestant Hospital Association
Leo M. Lyons, Executive Director
105 West Adams Street
Room 2035 Bankers Building,
Chicago 3, Illinois

American Public Welfare Association
Loula Dunn, Director
1313 East 60th Street
Chicago 37, Illinois

National Association for Mental Hygiene, Inc.
Richard P. Swigart, Executive Director
1790 Broadway
New York 19, N.Y.

Public Health Service
Dr. Leonard A. Scheele, Surgeon General
U.S. Department of Health, Education, and Welfare
Washington 25, D.C.

―――――――――◆―――――――――

Reading Materials

PENAL DIVISION

Focus. National Probation and Parole Association, 1790 Broadway, New York 19, N.Y. Bimonthly.

Manual of Suggested Standards for a State Correctional System. New York: American Prison Association, 1946.

Principles of Police Work with Minority Groups. Louisville, Kentucky: Louisville Division of Police, 1950. A manual adapted from *The Police and Minority Groups* by Dr. Joseph D. Lohman.

The Prison World. American Correctional Association and National Jail Association, 135 East 15th Street, New York 3, N.Y. Bimonthly publication.

Proceedings of the Annual Congress of Correction of the American Correctional Association, 135 East 15th Street, New York. Published annually.

Standards for Detention of Juveniles and Adults. Washington: Federal Security Agency. Community War Services Office. National Advisory Police Committee, Governmental Printing Office, 1945. FS 9.6:D 48.

Yearbook. New York: National Probation and Parole Association, 1790 Broadway, New York 19, N.Y. Annually.

Bates, Sanford. *Prisons and Beyond.* New York: The Macmillan Co., 1936.

Duffy, Clinton T. *The San Quentin Story.* Garden City: Doubleday and Co., 1950. This is the story of San Quentin as told to Dean Jennings by Warden Duffy.

Johnston, James A. *Alcatraz: Island Prison.* New York: Charles Scribner's Sons, 1949. The warden of Alcatraz presents a detailed story of this great prison.

Keller, Charles E., ed. *Helps for Grand Jurors in Kentucky.* Criminal Court Committee, Louisville Area Council of Churches, 1955. A booklet designed to instruct citizens called for grand jury service.

Kurtz, Russell H., ed. *Social Work Year Book.* New York: American Association of Social Workers. Published annually.

Lindner, Robert M. *Stone Walls and Men.* New York: Odyssey Press, 1946. The author has collected the facts about crime and criminals and presented them as a skillful observer and scientist.

Robinson, Louis N. *Jails: Care and Treatment of Misdemeanant Prisoners in the United States.* Philadelphia:

The John C. Winston Co., 1944. This work is an attempt to present a precise picture of the local penal institutions in the forty-eight states.

Scudder, Kenyon J. *Prisoners Are People.* Garden City: Doubleday and Co., 1952. The author presents an unembellished account of men in prison who are given an opportunity to regain their self-respect and to prepare constructively for the day of release.

CHILD-CARE DIVISION

Child. Children's Bureau of the United States Department of Health, Education, and Welfare, Washington 25, D.C. Bimonthly magazine.

Federal Probation. Administrative Office of U.S. Courts, Supreme Court Building, Washington 13, D.C. Quarterly.

Manual of Boys' Club Operation. New York: A. S. Barnes and Co., 1947.

Our Children Today. New York: Viking Press, 1952. Child Study Association of America, 132 East 74th Street, New York 21, N.Y.

The Proceedings. National Conference of Juvenile Agencies, Woodbine, New Jersey. Quarterly.

Allaman, Richard. "Human Relations at the Detention Home," *Federal Probation,* December, 1952.

———. "Managing Misbehavior at the Detention Home," *Federal Probation,* March, 1953.

Burmeister, Eva. *Forty-Five in the Family.* New York: Columbia University Press, 1949. The author tells the story of the Lakeside Children's Center in Milwaukee.

Deutsch, Albert. *Our Rejected Children.* Boston: Little, Brown and Co., 1950. Mr. Deutsch has written the story of juvenile delinquency. The account is based mainly on the author's coast-to-coast survey of so-called "reform schools," jails, and courts.

Hopkirk, Howard W. *Institutions Serving Children*. New York: Russell Sage Foundation, 1944.

McGovern, Cecelia. *Services to Children in Institutions*. National Conference of Catholic Charities, 1346 Connecticut Avenue, N.W., Washington 6, D.C., 1948.

Sherrill, Lewis J. *The Opening Doors of Childhood*. New York: The Macmillan Co., 1939.

Solomon, Ben. *Juvenile Delinquency—Practical Prevention*. Peekskill, New York: Youth Service, Inc., 1947.

Stern, Edith M., and Hopkirk, Howard W. *The House-mother's Guide*. Commonwealth Fund, Child Welfare League, 345 East 46th Street, New York 17, N.Y., 1946.

Teeters, N. K., and Reineman, J. O. *The Challenge of Delinquency*. New York: Prentice-Hall, Inc., 1950. A comprehensive discussion of all aspects of the problem of juvenile delinquency, including community action.

Vedder, Clyde B., ed. *The Juvenile Offender*. Garden City: Doubleday and Co., 1954. A collection of selected and valuable writings on delinquency problems.

HEALTH DIVISION

Bulletin. American Protestant Hospital Association, Station A, Box 7, Evansville 11, Indiana. Quarterly.

Hospitals. American Hospital Association, 18 Division Street, Chicago 10, Illinois. Monthly.

Bachmeyer, A. C., M.D., and Hartman, G. G. F., eds. *The Hospital in Modern Society*. New York: The Commonwealth Fund, 1943. The material is taken exclusively from periodical literature and from transactions and committee reports. Ninety-eight authors are represented by 145 articles.

Boisen, Anton T. *The Exploration of the Inner World*. New York: Harper & Bros., 1936. A pioneer study of the relations of mental disorder and religious experience.

Cabot, Richard C., M.D., and Dicks, Russell L., B.D. *The Art of Ministering to the Sick*. New York: The Macmillan Co., 1936. One of the older "modern" books written to aid all who care for the sick: doctors, nurses, social workers, ministers, and the sick themselves. A classic in its field.

Dicks, Russell L. *You Came Unto Me*. Department of Pastoral Care, Duke University, Box 4802, Durham, North Carolina, 1951. An inexpensive, practically useful manual for the training of hospital visitors.

Klein, D. B. *Mental Hygiene, the Psychology of Personal Adjustment*. New York: Henry Holt and Co., 1944. A discussion of the prevention of mental illness and the promotion of mental health.

MacEachern, Malcolm T. *Hospital Organization and Management*. Chicago: Physicians' Record, 1935.

McKenzie, John G. *Nervous Disorders and Religion*. London: George Allen and Unwin, Ltd., 1951.

Oates, Wayne E. *Religious Factors in Mental Illness*. New York: Association Press, 1955. A more recent elaboration and application of Boisen's hypothesis.

Prall, Charles E. *Problems of Hospital Administration*. Chicago: Physicians' Record Co., 1948. A report of a study based upon interviews with a hundred hospital administrators located in various parts of the United States.

Preston, George H., M.D. *Psychiatry for the Curious*. New York: Rinehart and Co., 1940. An interesting, accurate, but nontechnical introduction.

Stern, Edith M., and Hamilton, Samuel W., M.D. *Mental Illness: a Guide for the Family*. New York: The Commonwealth Fund, 1945. The authors give guidance to families of those who suffer mental illness.